4

THE DESIGNER'S GUIDE TO
SAMURAI
PATTERNS

JEANNE ALLEN

Original book concept
by Takashi Katano

THAMES AND HUDSON

■ INTRODUCTION

Last September, my friend Kazu and I were on our way to dinner in the Gion section of Kyoto when we came upon another friend, Nori-*san*. I had met Nori at Kazu's tennis club and knew he was the president of a large Japanese insurance company and an avid tennis player. Dressed in informal kimono, he was also headed for the Gion to attend tea ceremony instruction, which he had been studying for 14 years. He suggested that we meet later at the teahouse *(cha ya);* in the meantime, he would call a *maiko* (young geisha) whom we all knew to join us in a birthday celebration for Kazu.

We met as planned at the *cha ya* and were soon joined by the young geisha, a friend of Kazu's 19-year-old daughter, wearing a red-and-gold wide-sleeved kimono, a wig, and full white makeup. We chatted, drank champagne, and enjoyed the warm autumn evening from the wooden teahouse that has been in the pleasure business since Edo times. After an hour or so, the mama of the teahouse brought in the cellular telephone that summoned *maiko-san* to another *cha ya,* where a patron awaited her company. She left obediently, clopping away on wooden *geta* along the ancient stone streets to her next appointment.

The evening was a memorable glimpse into why the Japanese are so successful in perpetuating their complicated and exacting traditional culture. Nori-*san,* seriously studying the contemplative art of tea ceremony after long hours at the office, is a contemporary samurai. Without doubt, many of the ethical and aesthetic disciplines practiced by the samurai in the fourteenth century are still the standard today. The marketers of bestselling management books recognize this and liken the Japanese businessman —in his vassal-like relationship to his company—to his samurai ancestor. Miyamoto Musashi's *A Book of Five Rings—A Samurai Battle Strategy* is promoted as "... a guide for business practice ... how to run sales campaigns like military operations ... with the energy of the entrepreneurial Japanese businessman."

Apart from business, the samurai legend is kept alive within the popular culture. In Japan today, it is nearly impossible to turn on the television at any time of the day or night without encountering one or more samurai soaps. In these incredibly popular dramatizations that glorify the martial arts—along with the virtues of selfless devotion to duty and the willingness to die for one's lord— samurai values are replayed ad infinitum. To understand this phenomenon in another context, imagine that the tales of King Arthur or other medieval morality plays were the most popular form of TV entertainment in the United States. No wonder the samurai persists as Japan's greatest folk hero.

The word samurai comes from *saburau,* meaning "to serve." In the Heian period (794–1185), the samurai were military guards sent out by the imperial courts to subdue the increasingly strident provincial warriors. As Japan passed from the Golden Age of the Heian court into the Feudal Age of the shogun, the samurai rank was extended beyond the imperial court into the provinces and given to those warriors who held rank in service to their *daimyō* (feudal lord).

Minamoto Yoritomo, the first great shogun, can be credited with setting the standard as the ideal shogun—equal measure soldier, administrator, and poet. For the next seven hundred years, all shoguns would emulate him, including Tokugawa Ieyasu, who reunited Japan in the Edo period.

Yoritomo emerged from the Genji-Heike wars victorious. A leader with vision and resolve, he chose to distance himself from the decaying Heian society and moved his court to Kamakura, three hundred miles east of the capital. There he assumed the title of shogun—a contraction of *seiitaishogun,* meaning "great general who quells the barbarians." Finally out from under the imperial thumb, he developed the *bakafu,* a military government that assumed supreme authority throughout the empire. The hierarchy was supported by provincial lords—the *daimyō* and their armed retainers, the samurai. The "divine" emperor in Kyoto was no more than a figurehead, although Yoritomo always showed him respect and made it his official work to rebuild war-torn Kyoto.

The establishment of the Kamakura military seat marked the beginning of a time when samurai spirit and Yoritomo's creed of *bushidō*—the Way of the Warrior —ruled the country. This sacred code assumed patronage by the *daimyō* in return for military service from the samurai. Like the Arthurian code, *bushidō* meant unswerving loyalty.

In the beginning, Yoritomo's warriors were a motley lot drawn from the surrounding farms and thrown together with the barbarian warriors who had always been considered less than human by Kyoto's polite society. The first step in harnessing this native strength was to discipline the ranks through the teaching of the martial arts *(bu)* of archery, swordsmanship, hunting, and falconry. Yoritomo's *bakafu* ruled with spartan resolution and unyielding discipline; by 1333, Kamakura was a well-oiled military machine.

Having successfully secured the country's political and military power, Yoritomo's camp society had clearly become the nucleus of the post-Heian world. As the Kyoto court continued to flounder, the Kamakurans had to acquaint themselves with the previously scorned civilian and courtly arts *(bun).* Yoritomo's *bushidō* code was expanded to encourage a balance between *bu* and *bun. Daimyō,* who were first and foremost great swordsmen and falconers, came to be equally fine administrators with the literary skills necessary to govern their regional domains. Samurai developed the ability to consort with the cultured elite whom they were steadily displacing.

By the middle of the fourteenth century, samurai routinely joined literary gatherings, where they studied Chinese art and philosophy and composed verse. Calligraphy and ink painting were also avidly studied, as was *ikebana* (flower arranging). The restoration of the temples in Nara and Kyoto stimulated a renewed interest in the T'ang and Sung dynasties.

Throughout this cultural awakening, the ethic of simplicity in all things was strictly enforced. The elaborate dress of the Heian court was banished as vain and impractical. Instead, Kamakuran women wore uncomplicated garments like the *kosode*—a small-sleeved kimono that had been a modest undergarment in Heian dress. *Daimyō* and samurai were still expected to wear brocade robes for court occasions, but their patronage was not enough to keep the domestic weaving industry in Nishijin alive. By the Muromachi period (1338–1568), most of the brocades worn for court were imported at great expense from China, which once again exploited the Japanese passion for beautiful textiles.

Anticipating his court's weakness for personal adornments, Yoritomo passed strict sumptuary laws. Still, the Kamakurans quickly calculated that what was excluded in civilian dress could be included in military gear. The battle dress and trappings of the period were nothing less than works of art. While the weaving industry withered, the metalsmiths who made swords and helmets flourished. Battlecoats *(jin-baori)* and battle flags were made of silk and richly appliqued with gold and silver threads. The family crest *(mon)* took on major significance because it was used to decorate everything from armor to lacquerware. As samurai selected auspicious motifs and turned them into *komon* (miniature patterns) to decorate their possessions on and off the battlefield, civilians in and around the bustling castle-towns also procured *mon* to decorate their kimono, lacquerware, and ceramics. In spite of Yoritomo's efforts, the samurai period is

one of the most decorated in Japanese history.

This book of designs surveys the decorative motifs of the time. While the primary use of these patterns was for battle dress, the designs themselves are often notable for their delicacy and lyricism. The Kamakurans contributed the *mon* and its use in repeat as *komon* to Japanese decorative art history, but they also revived a studied enthusiasm for the Chinese arts, which had been banished by the self-absorbed Heians. The introduction from China of Zen Buddhism, the accompanying popularity of *chanoyu* (tea ceremony), and the development of Noh theater, which featured spectacular brocaded costumes, served to awe and inspire the Kamakuran court. The result was a military culture in form only. The keen appreciation and patronage of the shoguns, *daimyō,* and samurai created a legacy of intricately constructed and beautifully decorated armor, refined porcelain, rustic stoneware, portraiture, and sculpture—in all, a wealth of decoration that still stands as the pride of the Japanese culture.

Jin-baori (overjacket) decorated with the design shown in example 92.

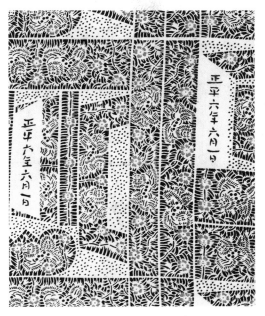

Cloth decorated with the lion design shown in example 84.

1

2

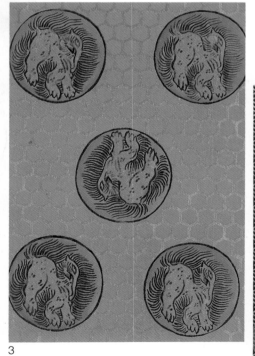

3

4

5

6

7

8

9

10

11

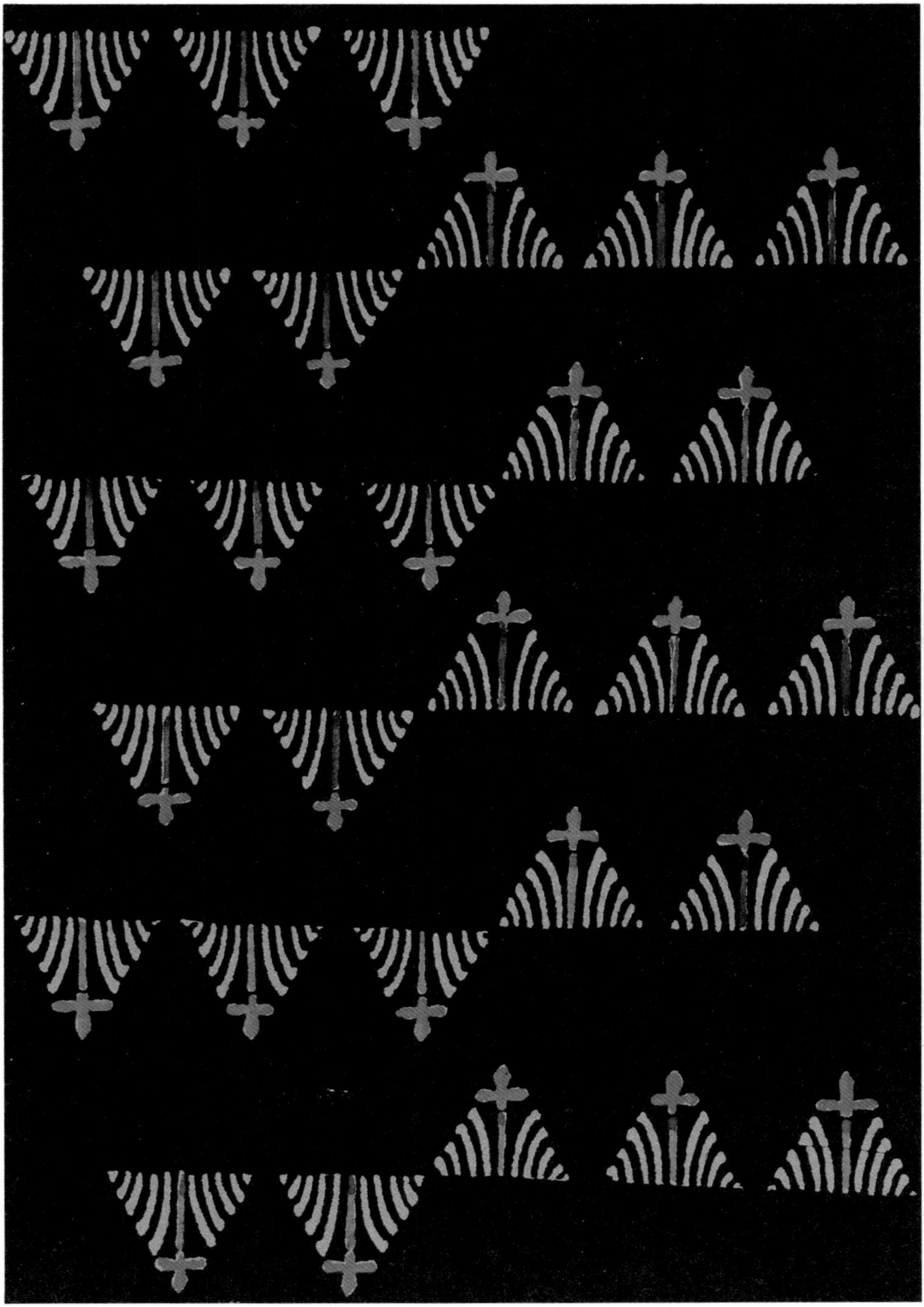
12

13

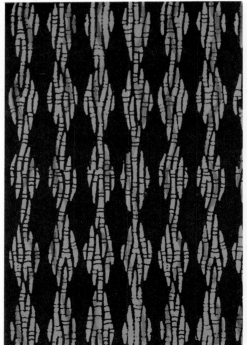

14

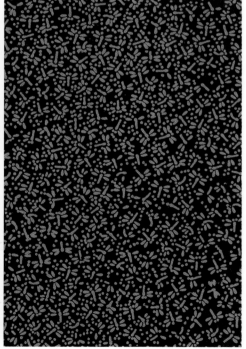

15

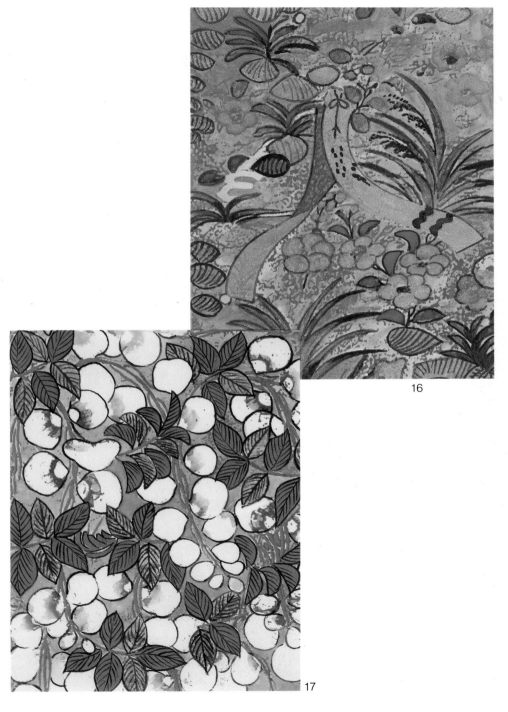

16

17

19

19 ■ Autumn Flowers

This delicate pattern decorated the leather helmet of famous samurai Minamoto Yoshitsune, brother of Shogun Yoritomo. The adventures of the two provide *monogatari* (heroic tales) that are comparable to the legends of King Arthur. Yoritomo eventually banished Yoshitsune and forced his brother's mistress, Shizuka, to dance before the court of Hachiman Shrine. Her performance is remembered for its purity, grace, and sadness, establishing her as the romantic heroine of the samurai period.

20 ■ Swallowtail Butterfly

In spite of constant civil war in the Muromachi period (1338–1568), respect for the classical arts re-emerged, and designs such as this Heian-inspired composition of butterflies delicately poised on autumn grasses were once again the style.

21 ■ Lattice Weave

During the Kamakura period (1185–1338), the weaving industry in Kyoto was nearly destroyed by civil strife. Most woven patterns were imported from China and therefore expensive, so printed faux weaves like this design of parallel crosses came into popular use.

22 ■ Scroll

This charming scroll design was inspired by the curly fiddlehead ferns that are gathered and eaten as a seasonal delicacy in the early spring. The design was often used by the Kaga artisans from central Japan to decorate their exquisite lacquerware.

23 ■ Plum Blossoms

The plum blossom pattern has always reigned as the most popular of motifs. It represents optimism because the appearance of the first plum blossom heralds the end of winter and the beginning of spring.

23

24

24 ■ Clouds and Dragons

The Kamakura period lasted for almost 150 years, and one of its greatest achievements was the creation of the samurai class. The same soldiers who were considered barely human by the overcultivated Heians came to personify the most highly esteemed values in Japanese culture. *Bushidō,* the Way of the Warrior, was a code of bravery, service, spartan living, and absolute loyalty. This design represents strength and typifies the kind of image the samurai chose to decorate clothing and personal possessions.

25

25 ■ Roundels and Double Butterflies

The butterfly is typical of the Japanese motifs that were popular during the Heian period (794–1185) and were revived during the lavish Muromachi. During this time, the Kanō School of art united the Chinese Sung-inspired aes-thetic and the distinctly Japanese *yamato* tradition of the Heians. In this carefully composed butterfly design, the Kanō School achieved the best of both worlds—a blend of Fujiwaran aristocratic refinement and Kamakura restraint.

26 ■ *Hanabishi* Roundels

This simple four-petal design was first used in early Noh costumes. During the Muromachi period, the Noh theater was the amusement of choice for Japan's ruling classes. The opulent brocades used in the costumes were initially imported from China, but became both impractical and expensive as the theater increased in popularity, with several troupes performing simultaneously. The consequence of this need was the revitalization of Kyoto's Nishijin weaving industry in the Momoyama period (1576–1603).

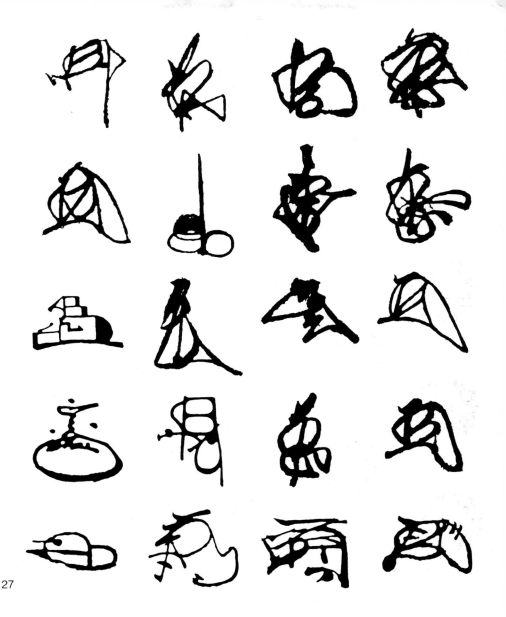

27

27 ■ Signature Pattern

In Japan, the *hanko* (seal) serves as an official signature. The samurai also used a *kaō* (written signature). Because the *bushidō* code demanded a cultivation of courtly arts, including calligraphy, tea ceremony, and *ikebana* (flower arranging), samurai signatures were often very beautiful; in the case of this design, some were beautiful enough to be used as textile designs.

28 ■ Japanese Oak
The pattern shown in this particularly graceful interpretation of the revered oak motif was often used to decorate samurai court dress. The oak represented strength and sturdy simplicity, values highly esteemed in Kamakuran military society.

29 ■ Water Wheels
The wheel has been a favorite motif throughout Japanese design history. Some of the popularity is due to its approximation of the roundel theme that was borrowed from China. Here, the wheel and the water flowing around it are mere suggestions—a kind of visual haiku.

30 ■ Flowers and Butterflies

The butterfly in this beautiful Kamakuran pattern is drawn in a simple, direct style typical of the time. What makes the design unusual is the asymmetrical arrangement of the *hanabishi* in roundels. A design of this sophistication was probably worn for ceremonial occasions.

31 ■ Dragonfly

The dragonfly, still associated with the samurai culture, was a metaphor for warrior life. In the larva state, the dragonfly appears to be wearing armor; later its colorful, showy body emerges from the armor and flies until captured by another insect.

32 ■ Win Bugs

The samurai called the dragonfly
katsumushi, meaning "win bug." In this
dramatic design, the fierce *katsumushi* is
engineered to decorate a samurai quiver.
The dragonfly is set out on a series of
segmented hexagons representing a
bamboo net. The quiver itself was
crafted of thin, lacquered bamboo strips
and was appreciated for its elegance.

33

33 ▪ Thunder

This kinetic design of ratcheted thunder-bolts was another favorite samurai pattern. Although now accepted as a natural phenomenon, thunder was perceived in samurai times as the wrath of the powerful thunder god and, as such, was to be treated with fear and respect. The samurai wore the pattern as a kind of insurance because they often were out in the open and at the mercy of the elements.

34 ■ *Karakusa*

Nailhead covers were usually made of copper by metal craftsmen. This magnificent work of *karakusa* (scrolling vines) was designed and executed by artisans attached to the Maeda clan in central Japan.

35 ■ **Irregular Scales**

The freshness of this modern-looking triangle design comes from its simple motif and the irregular arrangement of the design elements. It was probably used as a *kusube* design, in which the motif was transferred onto leather via a smoking process.

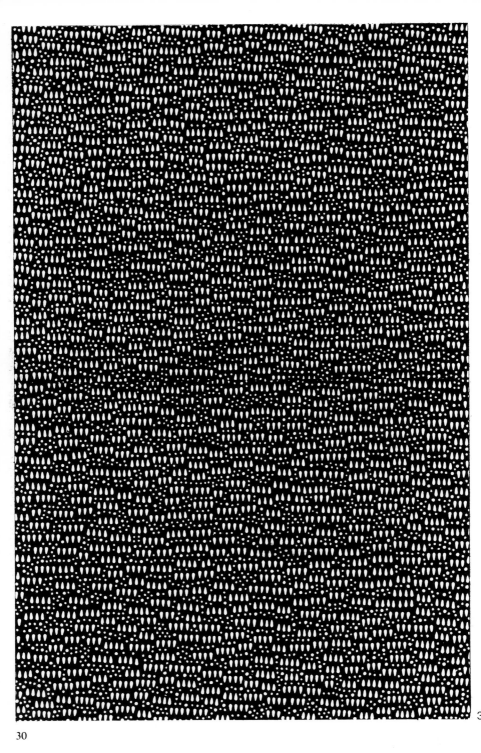

36

37

36 ■ Irregular Japanese Irises

Like the scale pattern, this design was originally created to decorate leather armor. The irises are abstracted into easily stenciled, pointed lobes. Despite its dizzy personality, the design was so popular that it was eventually transferred to cloth and allowed to enter the public domain.

37 ■ Irregular *Kinran* Pattern

This geometric pattern first appeared on the sumptuous brocaded cloaks worn over kimono for Kamakura and Muromachi court occasions. The textile was called *kinran*, a gold-patterned, plain-colored silk woven with paper-backed gold thread.

38 ■ Irregular Diamond

During the Muromachi period, the samurai adapted to the more lavish court life and wore silk coats made from imported brocade. The narrow sleeves of the coat were decorated with leather laces, and the back of the jacket was decorated with a large embroidered *mon*. The garment, appropriately, was named *diamon* (big crest). The *diamon* was worn with short pants under the samurai's armor in a combination known as *yoroi-hitatare*.

39 ■ Irregular Measure Pattern

Commonplace subjects have always been used by the Japanese to decorate their everyday working clothes. This pattern is just one example of the many measure designs that were a popular theme for Kamakuran textiles. Easy to print and within the popular domain, the square measure box was a pleasing motif when scattered across the cloth or stacked on end as in the famous *san-shō* pattern.

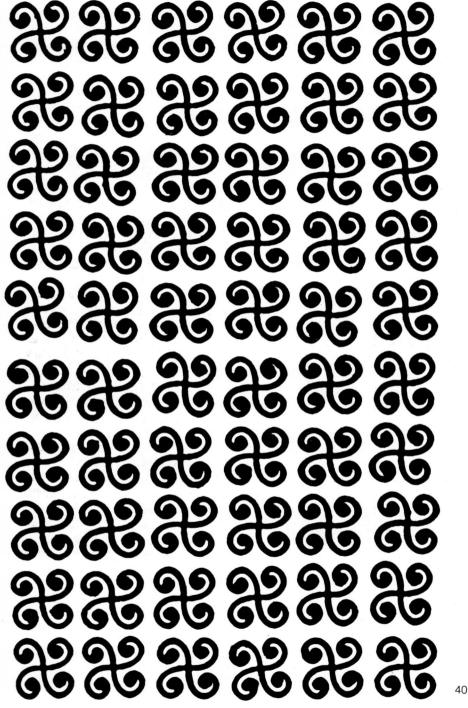

41

40 ▪ Irregular Swastika Pattern

The slightly askew positioning of this cheery little motif lifts it above the mundane. Although not obvious at first glance, the symbol used here is a swastika—originally an ancient Buddhist motif—crossed and curled in a remarkably modern stylization.

41 ▪ Chrysanthemums and Mist

The chrysanthemum pattern is often associated with the imperial family and, in fact, was reserved for their exclusive use at different times in Japanese history. The samurai also chose a personal *mon* that was used to decorate both their court and battle dress.

42 ■ **Chrysanthemums in Roundels**

This charming stripe is composed of rows of *kugi-kakushi*, decorative coverings for nailheads in wooden houses. Skillful Japanese carpenters did not use nails in their best work—the greatest example of their craftsmanship is Kyoto's Kiyomizu Temple, built without a single nail.

43 ■ **Scattered Tortoise Shells**

The turtle was a favorite samurai totem. Revered for its restorative powers and longevity, the tortoise has also been a Japanese culinary delicacy since ancient times. In this design, the turtle's shell is abstracted and laid out in a fresh, simple pattern.

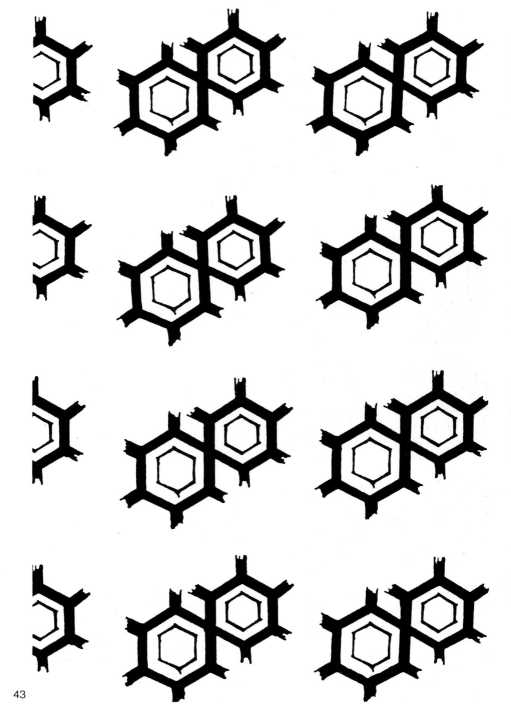

44 ■ *Kiri* (Paulownia)

Known as *go san no kiri* (five, three of
paulownia), this version of the paulownia
pattern is one of the most famous
designs of the samurai period. It graced
Hideyoshi's battlecoat when the great
samurai general united Japan in the late
sixteenth century.

45 ■ Paulownia in Roundels and Lattices

Here, the paulownia motif is styled for
the silk brocade of a Noh robe or for the
silver and gold *maki-ē* used to decorate a
lacquer piece. The design is known as *go
shichi no kiri* (five, seven of paulownia),
which signifies the number of flowers on
each stem.

46 ■ Paulownia and *Karakusa*

This delicate Chinese-inspired design probably originated as a brocade woven in the *karakusa* (scrolling vine) pattern with the paulownia motifs embroidered over the top in gold and silver threads. The Japanese weaving industry was seriously affected by the civil war during this period. In the Momoyama period, however, imported Chinese silks restimulated Kyoto's dormant Nishijin weaving industry. Always in demand, richly embellished fabrics such as these were an essential part of samurai court dress.

47

47 ■ Scattered Clouds

This quirky pattern of curly clouds skittering across the picture plane was borrowed from the Chinese and incorporated into the Japanese iconography. The Muromachi period, which lasted almost two and a half centuries, was a time of devastating civil war, but it was also an era of lavish art patronage. As contemporaries of the leaders of China's glorious Ming dynasty, the Muromachi shoguns brought Chinese ceramics and textiles to Japan, where they were admired and openly imitated.

48 ■ Sword and Clouds

Typical of the kind of bold graphic that might decorate the *jin-baori* of a Kurosawa samurai, this image of a sword thrust through clouds was adapted from a famous Buddhist design. In the original, Amida Nyorai stands on a similarly stylized cloud. Many samurai were deeply committed to Zen Buddhism, whose strict religious tenets perfectly suited the austere lifestyle of the warrior.

49

49 ▪ Lattices and Melons

This apparently innocent design of leaves and waxed gourds entwined on a latticed background actually held important political significance. The hollyhock leaves signalled that whatever the design adorned was the exclusive prop-erty of the mighty Tokugawa family, the shogunate that established Edo, the military encampment now known as Tokyo. This design was initially crafted in metal and made into an ornament that was part of a samurai's furnishings.

50 ■ Bamboo Grass

This simple design of bamboo grass set into roundels is typical of the spare but elegant brushwork that was esteemed during the Kamakura period. The introduction of Zen Buddhism to Japan brought with it an admiration for the austere calligraphy of China's Sung dynasty, which was widely emulated in Japanese Zen monasteries.

51

51 ■ Chinese Dragons

The samurai adopted animal images to express the characteristics they aspired to. Predictably, one of the favorite choices was the mythological dragon, embodying the ferocity and strength the warriors needed in battle. This very old and beautiful design of the dragon was used to decorate a warrior's personal lacquerware. Here, the etched image of the restless dragon thrusts through eddies of stylized clouds and banks of peonies.

52

53

52 ■ **Midwinter Hollyhocks**

This innocuous pattern became politically significant in the seventeenth century when the Tokugawa shogunate came to power. Tokugawa Ieyasu chose the hollyhock as his family crest, admiring the plant for its hardiness and its reflection of the spartan samurai lifestyle.

53 ■ *Tsujigahana-Zome*

The imagery for these delicate bouquets was achieved through the stitched tie-dyeing process known as *tsujiganaha-zome*. This process was often used in conjunction with indigo dyeing to produce the distinct textile designs we identify as *mingei* (Japanese country style).

54 ▪ **Paulownia and a Chinese Phoenix**

The paulownia and the phoenix were among the most powerful symbols in ancient Japan. Most popularly used in the crests adopted by the samurai, these two images were also used in conjunction with the image of bamboo to decorate the emperor's ceremonial robes. In this simple sketch, the artist is presenting, not a composed design, but two motifs set down in a pretty and unpretentious manner.

55

55 ■ Chinese Bellflower and Paulownia

These simple graphic florals are samurai crests. Although this particular composition was probably done in gold for a lacquer wedding box, the images usually appeared individually. The use of the crests can be traced back to pre-Heian times. Not until the Kamakura period, however, were the crests used on the battlefield as a means of discerning friends from enemies.

56 ■ **Bamboo and Cranes**

Because the crane mates for life, its elegant form is often used to decorate the wedding kimono of a new bride. In this design, the crane rises through the bamboo preparing to take flight into the bright blue skies of the future.

57 ■ **Basketweave and Crabs**

In the Kamakura period, domestic and workday items became acceptable subject matter for artists and craftsmen. This design shows a latticework *jakago* (crab basket trap), which is filled with stones and dropped into the river to trap the evening's dinner.

58 ▪ Scales and Crests

In the Kamakura period, many of the *mon* (crests) that served a practical purpose on the battlefield were adopted by noble families for domestic use. Here, the crests scattered across the scale pattern were probably embroidered in gold, silver, and silk threads.

59 ▪ Boxes, Fans, and Flowers

Kamakuran style was austere compared with that of the flamboyant Fugiwaras. Still, the shogunate had to wear elaborately decorated outerrobes for ceremonial occasions. This pattern, originally embroidered onto a court garment, was later used to decorate a screen.

60 ■ *Kome* (Rice) Lattices

This eclectic lattice design is the kind of visual riddle that became a popular artistic device during the Edo period (1603–1868). The starlike motif is actually a stylized version of the *kanji* ideograph for the word *kome* (rice). First used by the Date clan from Sendai in the north of Japan, the pattern was widely admired for its cleverness and design integrity.

61 ■ **Small Flowers** This simple blockprinted design has a delicate clarity common to many *komon* patterns.

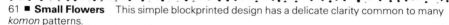

62 ■ **Flower Squares** The irregularities caused by the artist's carving give this design its interesting character.

61–82 ■ *Komon*

Examples 61 through 82 show *komon*—small, over-all patterns that became an important genre of decoration during the Kamakura period. Closely associated with the samurai, the designs were initially used to decorate the leather pieces lining the warrior's armor. Known as *ekawa*, this leatherwork was usually

painted or branded with the samurai's personal *komon*. This inside leather was soft and supple, while the arrow-repelling outer shell of armor was made of overlapping lacquer plates strung together with resilient cording. The samurai usually selected a *komon* as a

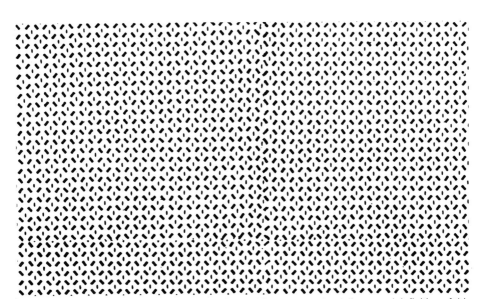

63 ■ **Diagonal Squares** The strong, clear diagonal lines assure the delicacy and definition of this design.

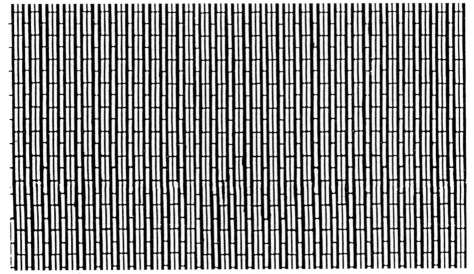

64 ■ **Bamboo Fence** The personality of this bamboo stripe is maintained by artful placement of the irregular horizontal lines.

visual metaphor for a desirable characteristic or physical attribute—a quality that offered inspiration or protection during battle.

The samurai were heroes to the citizens in the castle towns. All things comprising samurai culture, including the small *komon* designs, were taken up by the local populations. The simplicity of *komon* made them easy and inexpensive to adapt to textile printing, and they were soon decorating townsmen's kimono.

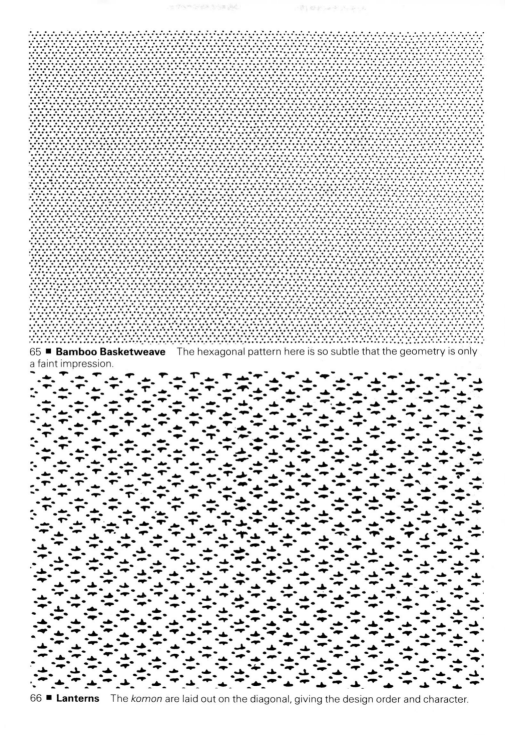

65 ■ Bamboo Basketweave   The hexagonal pattern here is so subtle that the geometry is only a faint impression.

66 ■ Lanterns   The *komon* are laid out on the diagonal, giving the design order and character.

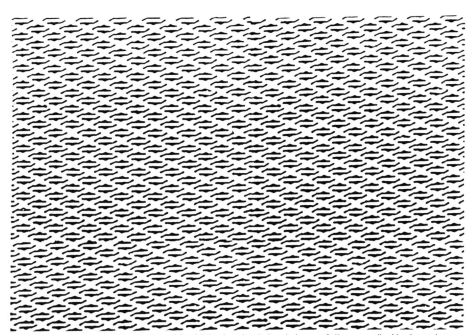

67 ■ **Clouds** This lyrical design of Buddhist-inspired clouds is carefully controlled by its strict diagonal layout.

68 ■ *Shoji-Gumi* *Shoji* (paper screens that divide Japanese rooms) inspired this design of three horizontal lines and opposed squares.

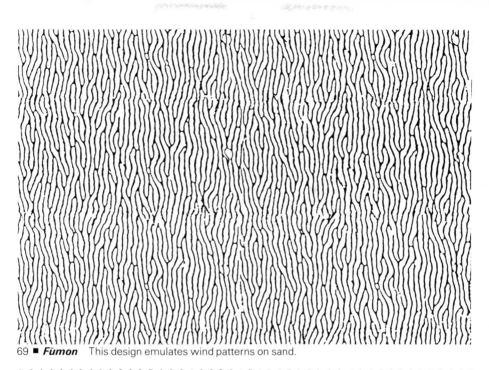

69 ■ *Fūmon*   This design emulates wind patterns on sand.

70 ■ **Box Forms**   This is not an op-art riddle from the sixties, but you could connect the lines to create 3-D boxes.

71 ■ *Mijin* This seemingly random "broken to pieces" design actually has a definite, if hard-to-find, repeat.

72 ■ Tortoise Shell If you connect the apparent flower points, the hexagons of the turtle shells appear.

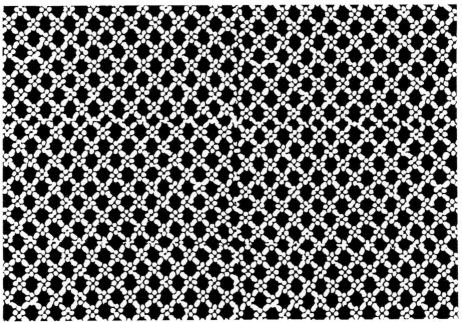

73 ■ **Net Pattern**   The irregularity of hand-tied knots in a fishing net inspired this design.

74 ■ *Noshi*   *Noshi*, abstracted here, is an auspicious symbol used to decorate gifts in Japan.

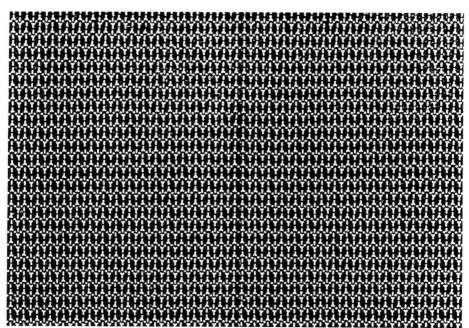

75 ■ **Arrow Feathers** A popular samurai design difficult to identify until the name is known.

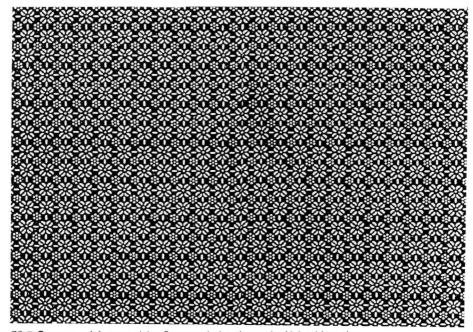

76 ■ **Sesame** A famous *daimyō* pattern belonging to the Nabeshima clan.

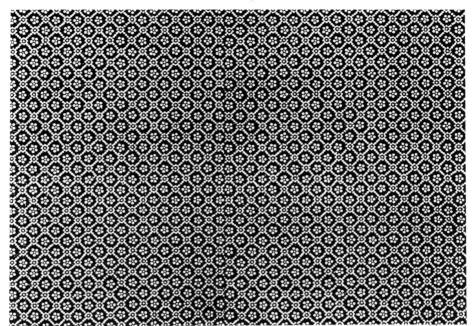

77 ■ **Plum Blossoms** An aristocratic design admired for its balance between delicate subject matter and geometric form.

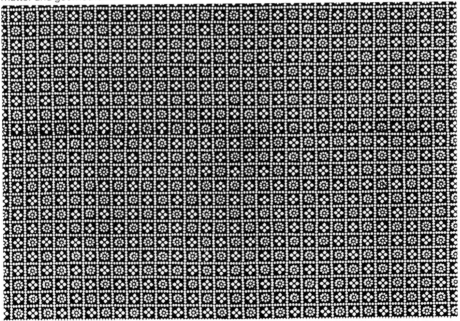

78 ■ **Crests** Alternating diamond and chrysanthemum crests are enclosed in fine-dot lattices.

79 ■ **Chicks**   An amusing pattern of overlapping chicks, distinctly Edo in subject and technique.

80 ■ **Arms**   Bamboo swords, masks, and spears are punched out in this flurry of practice armaments.

81 ■ *Tomaya* *Tomaya* (rush-thatched cottages) sitting in the sand by the sea.

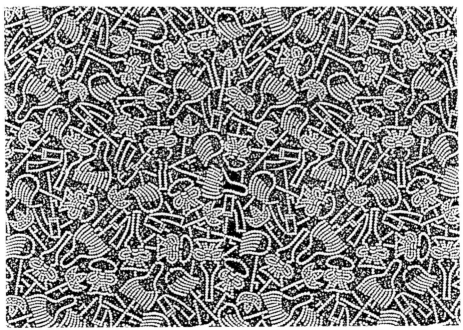

82 ■ *Daimyō* **Procession** Symbols carried to announce the coming of a *daimyō* procession, a great display of wealth and power.

83

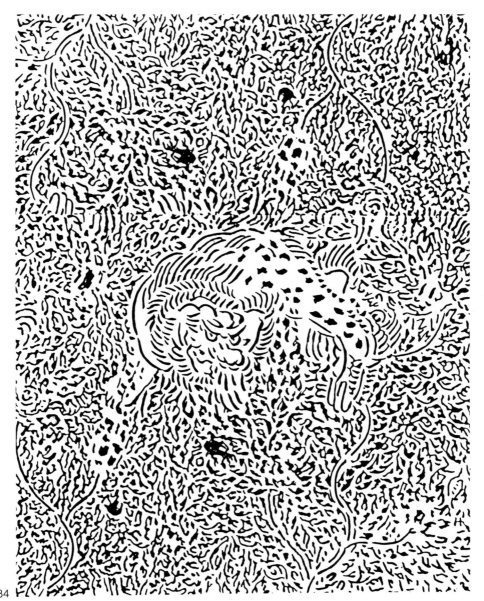

84

83 ■ *Komon* Stripe
This beautiful *komon* stripe decorated the inside of a samurai's armor where it was hidden from view. While simplicity and spartan virtues were the rule, the love of finery persisted and personal decoration continued to be worn in such clandestine ways.

84 ■ Lions
Because of constant warfare during the Kamakura period, warriors were rarely out of their armor. This design originally decorated a samurai helmet, most of which carried images representing courage or ferocity, such as the lion.

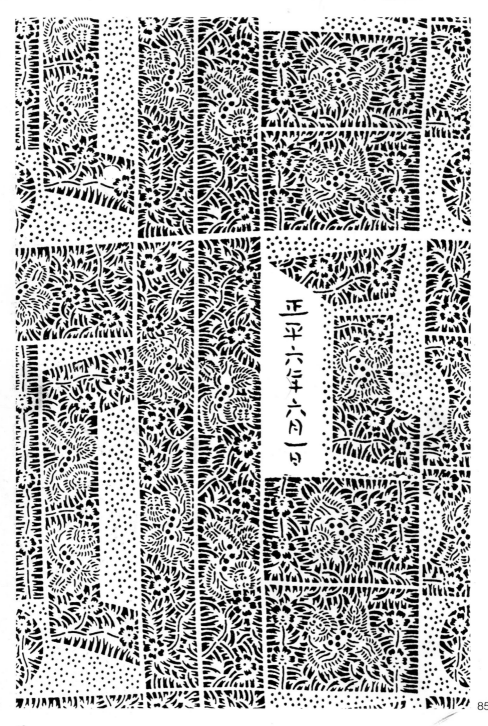

正平六年十六月一日

85

86

85 ■ Lions and Flowers
This leather design was created by using a process called *kusube*. After the design was drawn, exposed areas were smoked to a darker color. This kind of leather stenciling was specific to the Kamakura period.

86 ■ Stripes and *Mitsu-Domoe*
Mitsu-domoe (three comma shapes) are worked into a roundel and set into an *ichimatsu* (checked pattern) in this dramatically graphic pattern. This type of Noh theater design anticipates the even more dramatic Kabuki costumes to come in the Edo period.

87 ■ Crosses

Designs with Christian references were outlawed during the Edo period when the Tokugawa shogunate banned all vestiges of Christianity from Japan. This design of Western origin predates Tokugawa and is preserved in the Entsū Temple.

88 ■ Irises

A favorite samurai pattern, irises came to be associated with the warrior and his armor. Some of this appeal was probably due to its simplicity. Especially in abstract form, the iris was an easy image to paint or stencil onto leather using the *kusube* method.

89 ■ *Daimyō Mon*

This pattern shows 20 *daimyō mon* (feudal lord crests), symbols that grew in importance during this age as family clans began to replace the imperial court as the foundation of society. The crests, characterized by their graphic clarity, were either embroidered or appliqued onto cloth. Initially, the *daimyō* used symbols to identify clans during battle. Later, the feudal lords placed their *mon* on all possessions to display their wealth and power.

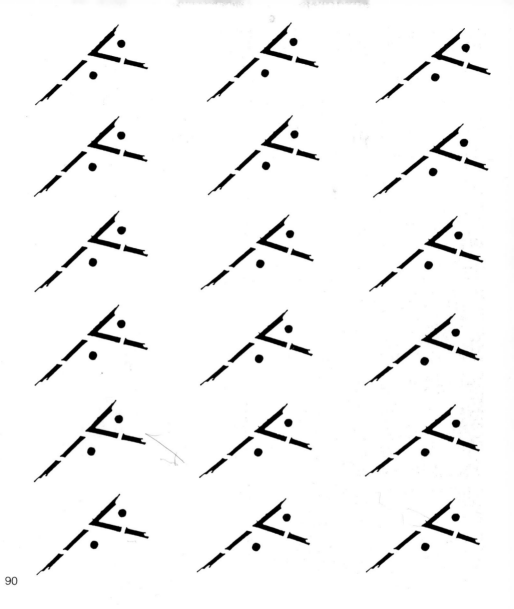

90 ■ Bamboo and Dewdrops

With just a few strokes of the brush, this minimalist pattern of crossed bamboo punctuated with dewdrops is executed with power and grace. Such abstract work embodied the aesthetic ideals of the Muromachi period. Artists of the Kanō School, influenced by the Sung painters in China, produced the most renowned Japanese painting of the time. Admired for the impressionistic beauty of its work, this influencial family was esteemed for its visual distillation of Zen ideals.

92

91 ■ *Tachibana* (Wild Oranges)
The Momoyama period coincided with a time of great European rulers, including Elizabeth I, Henry IV, and Philip II, enthusiastic supporters of foreign exchange. Flowing designs such as this were admired by the Europeans, taken home, and imitated by Western artists.

92 ■ Date Crest and Dots
Warriors of the Date clan were famous for their showy apparel both on and off the battlefield. Here the Date crest is shown over a field of dots. The design was colored in red, blue, and yellow— producing what has been described as an "intimidating effect" on the battlefield.

93

94

93 ■ *Chigai Taka-No-Ha* (Alternating Hawk Feathers)

This dramatic design of boldly drawn hawk feathers on a field of delicate snow flakes is an excellent example of *bu/bun* (juxtaposition of opposites)—a key to samurai mentality.

94 ■ Moon and Japanese Pampas Grasses

This elegant design is typical of the spare but moody paintings that often decorated the samurai's *fubako* (personal letter box). The heavy beauty of an autumn moon is balanced by the slender wisps of pampas grasses.

95 ■ **Moons**

This stamped-out version of moons and grasses was designed in the Kamakura period, when the *mon* (family crest) became a badge of recognition and an important design element. Roughly concurrent with the rise of heraldry in Europe, family crests were adopted by Japanese clans and decorated everything from battle flags to lacquerware. *Mon*, still used today, are often inherited. For families without samurai connections, crests can be purchased from dealers representing thousands of designs.

96

96 ■ Love Letters on Bushes

When Shogun Yoritomo established his
camp at Kamakura, members of the
court fell on hard times. The emperor
was often so destitute that he sold off
imperial treasures to survive. The
samurai, who began as an uncouth lot,
were decidedly not destitute and began
to be educated by the courtiers in calligraphy, *ikebana*, poetry, literature, and tea
ceremony. The samurai adopted many of
the arts, including writing short love
poems on paper, which was then folded
and tied to bushes, as shown in this
design.

98

97 ■ Grasses and Butterflies

In this feminine design, perky butterflies alight among the summer grasses in the early morning dew. Such classically "pretty" Heian patterns were brought into the Kamakura period, even though the Kamakurans preferred *wabi*, a sadder beauty.

98 ■ *Tori Kabuto*

Inspired by the crownlike head of the mythical phoenix, this design was used for *gagaku* (traditional court music) of the samurai period. The phoenix had been a popular image since Nara times (710–794), and variations of the image were eventually used to fashion warrior helmets.

99

100

99 ■ Waves
This dramatic design of negative/positive diamond *mon* above a surge of foaming sea was commissioned by a great warrior to decorate the back of his *jin-baori*. The power and sureness of the samurai is convincingly expressed in this still-modern design.

100 ■ Waves with Pine Trees and Plum Blossoms
This design of intertwined pine and plum blossoms set against the classical *seigaiha* (wave) pattern, was originally used to decorate a Noh robe. Sophisticated and feminine, the design is still used in *obi*.

101

101 ■ Double Lattices

Oddly enough, some of the most distinctive and popular Japanese patterns had their origins in architecture. This lattice design was probably created by an artisan whose daydreams fixed on the *gō-tenjō* (ceiling lattices) that roofed his workplace. The beautifully crafted wooden ceilings that are most often found in Shinto shrines were structured by crossing squared timbers on the diagonal. As in this pattern, intersection points were painted white and the interior space left pristinely blank.

84

102

103

104

105

102–105 ■ Four *Jin-Baori* (Overjackets)
Pictured here are four styles of *jin-baori* worn by the samurai to battle. These flamboyant garments featured the warrior's *mon* (personal totem). Elaborately appliqued and embroidered in brilliantly colored spun-silk thread, each *mon* was selected to inspire courage and bravery in the heat of battle. The disadvantage of such personalized decoration was that the enemy could easily identify individual warriors and proceed accordingly.

106 ■ Sword Guards

The samurai's sword was his most precious possession and was believed to have spiritual powers. Like other clan treasures, swords were held sacred by the samurai family and were handed down from generation to generation. If the sword was given up, it was usually endowed to a Shinto shrine, but never sold. The sword guards shown here protected the samurai's hand in battle. Because metalsmiths were among the great artisans of the period, the guard was itself a work of art.

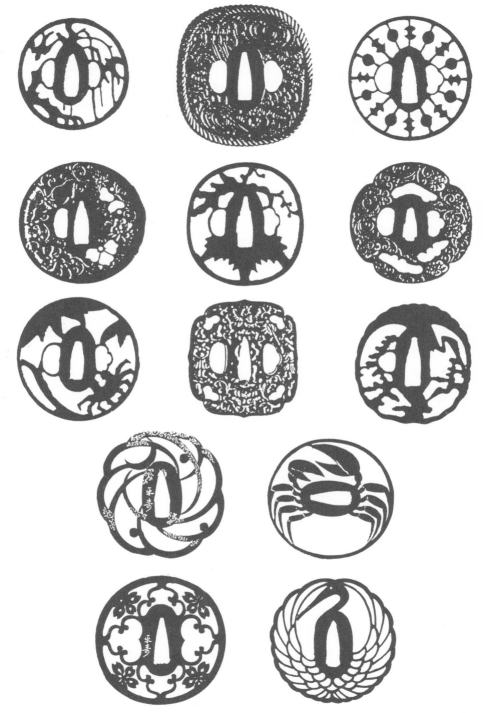

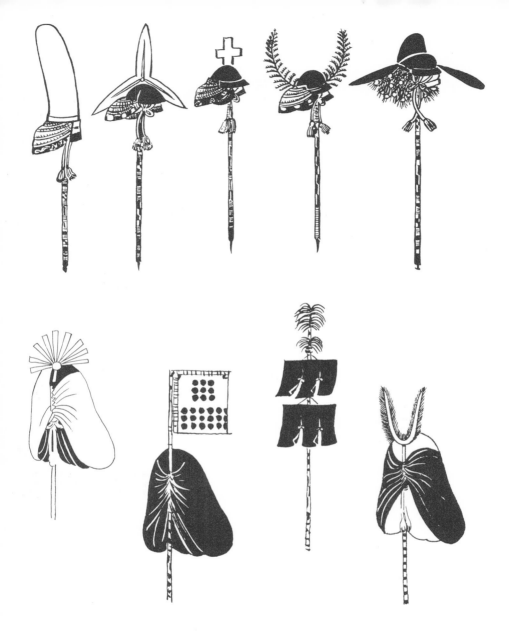

107 ■ Flags and War Ornaments

During the civil war period, beautiful *hata-sashimono* (war ornaments) were designed to intimidate the enemy and inspire the samurai. It was typical of the age that the most spectacular craftsman-ship was dedicated to the art of war. These meticulously crafted and beauti-fully decorated ornaments are now used for peaceful purposes, usually to decorate Shinto shrines.

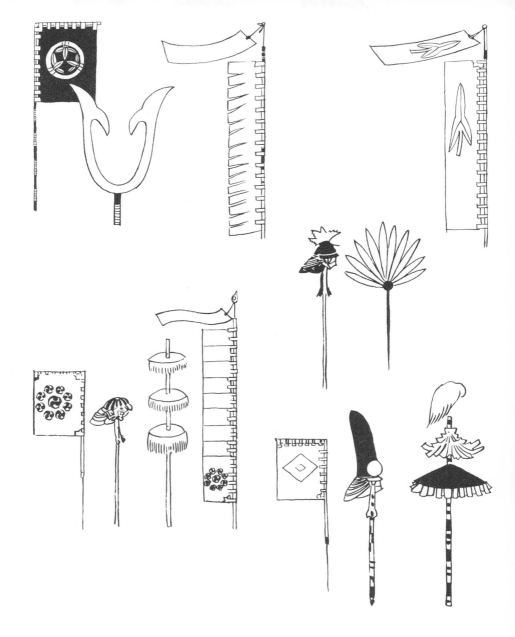

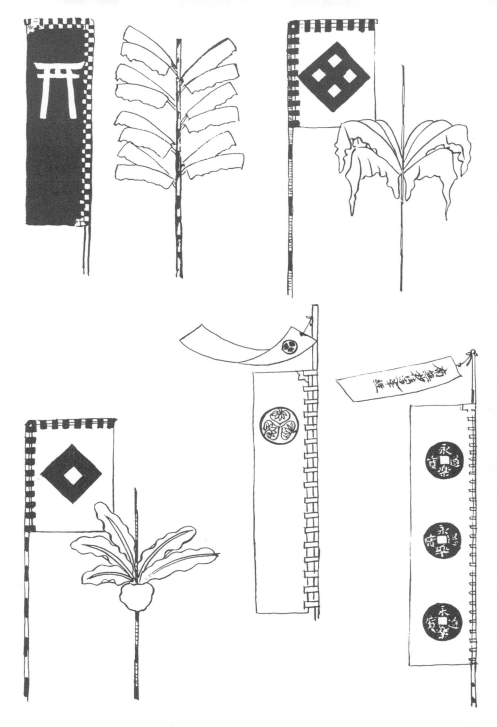

108 ■ Helmets

Next to his sword, the samurai's most valuable possession was his helmet. A warrior spent so much time in battle that his helmet became his protector in more than just an armored sense. Each helmet was decorated with the samurai's personal totem—dragons, bats, and other beings with symbolic powers. Most helmets were made of metal, leather, and lacquer, and their ability to endure battle has also preserved them through the ages. Many of those remaining are appreciated as works of art.

109 ■ *Hagi* (Bushclover)

This refreshingly simple pattern of bush-clover flowers and leaves was favored by Kamakuran women and children to decorate their everyday kimono. Such uncomplicated and modest designs were considered politically correct for the times, which had traded the gaudy excesses of the late Heian period for a value system that esteemed the qualities of austerity and restraint.

110 ■ Flower *Karakusa*
This delicate flower design set into roundels originated as a brocade imported at great expense from China by a warrior family. Because of its value, the family appropriated it for their exclusive use—as a textile and to decorate their furniture and personal accessories as well.

111 ■ Tokugawa *Hanabishi*
In this cleverly composed design belonging to the great Tokugawa clan of Edo, the *ichimatsu* (checked) pattern was achieved by setting the flower-shaped diamond (*hanabishi*) into the center of the roundels and then squaring off the composition with *karakusa* motifs.

111

112 ■ **Flower Diamond Vines**

Elegant scrolling designs such as this
were borrowed from expensive Chinese
brocades. As *chanoyu* (tea ceremony)
became more popular, tiny bits of the
brocade were used to wrap the tea
accessories, assuring that not an inch of
the fabric was wasted.

113 ■ **Half Moons and Plum Blossoms**

It was characteristic of Japanese design
to contrast symmetry and asymmetry.
Here, the half moon slices are presented
in an upright symmetrical style, while
spare plum branches bearing a few early
blooms cut across the flat moon plane.

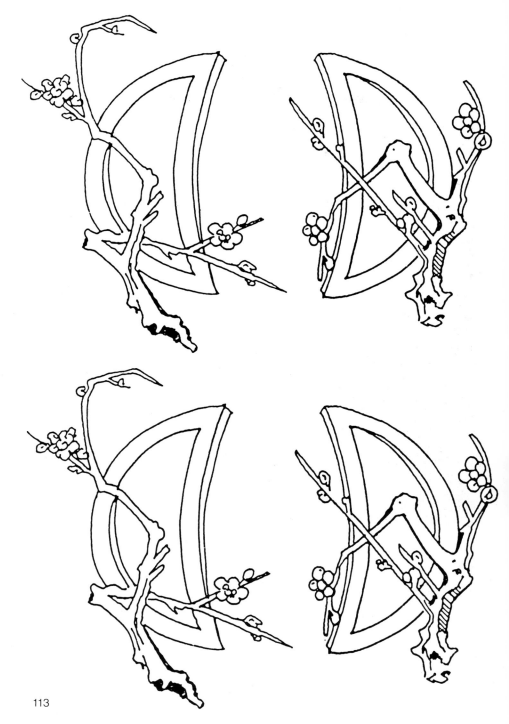

114

114 ■ Sailing Ship

The arrival of Portuguese sailing ships in the 1540s made a deep impression on everyone who saw them. This rather naively drawn ship design was probably commissioned by a samurai warrior and engineered to decorate the back of his *jin-baori*.

115 ■ Stacked Diamonds

This is another of the popular measure patterns, where the *masu* (wooden measuring boxes) are stacked to form a diamond pattern. This design was first printed on cloth and later adapted to decorate lacquerware and metalwork.

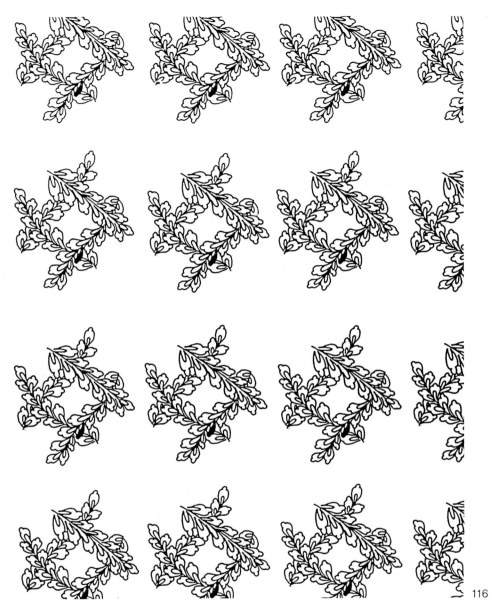

116 ■ *Fuji Igata*

This beautiful wisteria pattern is worked into rhythmic configurations of parallel crosses. Popular for women's kimono during the samurai period, this design can be seen in the scroll paintings of the day, which were known for their realism. The influence of China's Sung dynasty on Kamakuran art further encouraged realism, particularly in sculpture. For the first time, physical features were accurately recorded in the likenesses of the important shoguns, such as Yoritomo, and the Zen priests of the period.

117

117 ▪ Scrolling Wisteria

Brocades with decorative designs such as this graceful wisteria pattern were often used for tea ceremony, popularized when Zen Buddhism was brought to Japan from China. The drinking of tea (*chanoyu*) incorporated the Zen aesthetic of cultured rusticity known as *wabi*, and its popularity spread from the monasteries to the court. Although the trappings of the tea ceremony appear austere and ordinary, they are expensive accessories crafted by masters working within stringent guidelines.

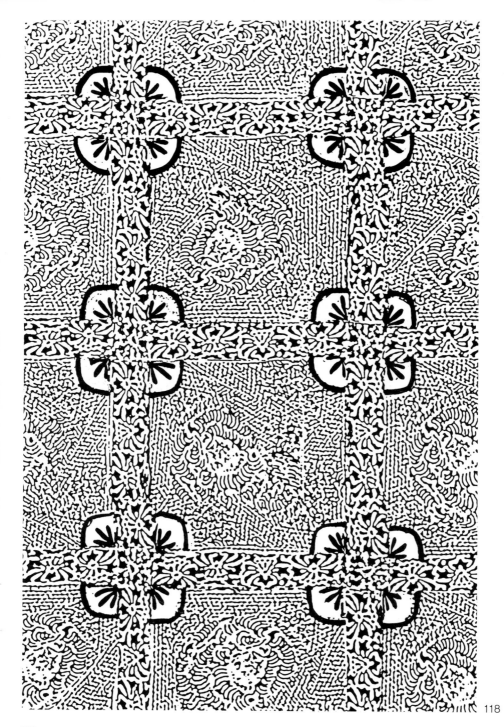

119

118 ■ Peonies

The decoration of swords, armor, helmets, and horse gear reached its technical and artistic peak in the samurai period. The peony in this lattice design was drawn to suggest a lion's head and was adapted to decorate a warrior's helmet.

119 ■ Pine Tree Branches

Traditionally, the pine branch is used to decorate the Noh stage. Originally danced outdoors or in Shinto shrines, Noh theater still uses simple staging today. The rich brocades worn by the actors make a striking contrast with the austerity of the sets.

120 ▪ Diamond Pine Tree Bark and Autumn Flowers

This samurai family pattern first used to decorate a woman's kimono shows a typically Japanese composition of autumn symbols (maple leaves, bush-clover, pampas grass) scattered against elongated diamond shapes.

121 ▪ Pine Bark

The mood of this design differs greatly from the romantic mood of the previous design. Comparing the two reveals the breadth of interpretation a single theme could inspire in the samurai period. Here, the masculine diamond shapes are angular yet still soft.

121

122

122 ■ Pine Trees and Waves from the Blue Ocean

Designed to decorate a Noh costume, this elegant pattern combines two classic Japanese themes: *seigaiha* (waves from the blue ocean) and pine trees. Most Noh plays center on a dramatic encounter between a troubled spirit and a priest.

123 ■ Pine Needles in Diamonds

This scattered and seemingly random design of pine needles on a diamond ground was first used in the Noh theater. Initially, Noh was danced by the priests, but during the Kamakura period, the theater was taken up by professional travelling troupes.

123

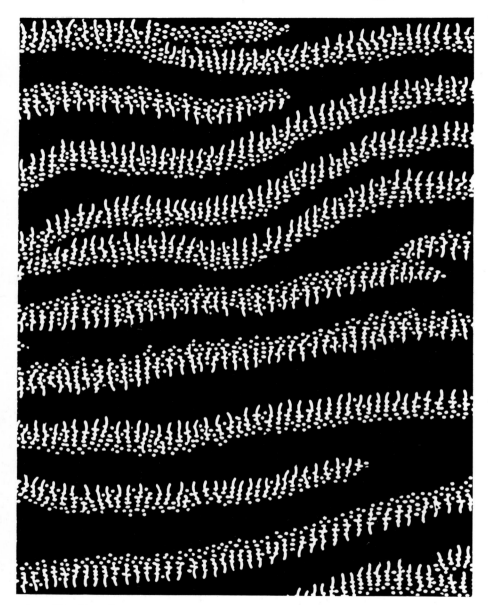

124 ■ **Pine Tree Grove**
Rhythmic and abstract, this design is a wandering stripe (*tatewaku*) composed of row upon row of tiny pine trees. The samurai often chose this stripe to decorate their everyday clothing, and it is still used to decorate summer *yukata* (lightweight robes).

125 ■ **Pine Tree Mountain**
Using evergreen as an armor decoration was popular among the samurai, who hoped the pine would bring them long life. The pine tree image in this design is placed within each mini-mountain. The mountains are worked in opposition to create a scale pattern.

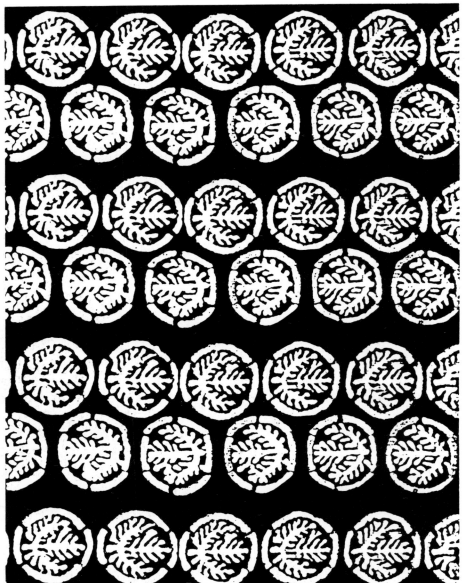

126 ■ Cedar Leaves in Roundels

Although the citizens of the castle towns could not afford the beautiful imported brocades worn at court, they adopted loose facsimiles of the patterns. This design is a simplification of a Chinese pattern and, for its own purposes, is as charming as the original.

127 ■ Water Birds and Waves

Profoundly influenced by the clear-sighted Zen view of the world, Kama-kuran artists painted images like this dramatic bird—imagery so realistic and drawing style so precise that even the distance between the birds and the waves is clearly described.

127

128

128 ■ Three-Leafed Hollyhocks

This lyrical design, preserved in Entsū Temple, is credited to the Tokugawa shogunate, who adopted the humble hollyhock for their family pattern. In 1600, the Tokugawas moved the capital of Japan from Kyoto to a swampland called Edo (present-day Tokyo). In an attempt to get away from the complications of court life and to recreate the spartan life of the Kamakura, Tokugawa Ieyasu reestablished a military-style camp that operated on the tenets of *bushidō*.

129

129 ■ Knotted Letters

The samurai and their loves exchanged messages and poems written on beautiful handmade papers (*washi*) that they folded and knotted into shapes like the ones in this romantic pattern. Here, paired chrysanthemums, symbolizing two lovers, are printed onto the poetry papers. A design like this one might have been used to decorate a samurai woman's *obi*.

130

130 ■ Melon Flowers

By the sixteenth century, castle-building had reached its zenith in Japan. Visiting Portuguese missionaries were awed by the beauty and architectural sophistication of the medieval wooden and stone structures. Although the interiors of the castles were austere, perfection was so important that the sight of an exposed nailhead was unacceptable. This delicate roundel pattern is adapted from a *kugi-kakushi* (nailhead covering) that might have been found in a shogun's castle or a samurai's residence.

131

131 ■ Wax Gourd Flowers

Here is another pattern inspired by *kugi-kakushi*. In the center of the roundels, leaves and vine tendrils surround wax gourd flowers. At the perimeter of the design, ears of rice create a wreath around the flowers and leaves. *Kugi-kakushi* were used to cover nailheads and sliding-door knobs as well. Many of these doors (*fushima*), painted by the masters of the Kanō and Tosa schools, were works of art in themselves. These artists are still revered for their expressive brushwork and sumptuous use of color.

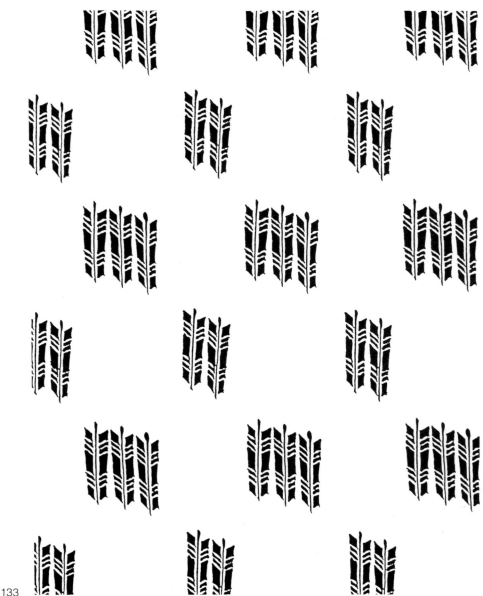

133

132 ■ Moon Flowers

This slightly eccentric pattern features the nuts of the moon flower. Within the nut pod are small flowers positioned like *shippō* (linked gems). The design is an auspicious one that suggests that its use will bring riches.

133 ■ Arrows

In the samurai era, tales of military heroism were carried by travelling priests and minstrels and were played out in Noh and Kyōgen theater. Patterns with military motifs were popular among village folk, who made heroes of their favorite warriors.

134 ■ Snow

During the Muromachi period, traditional Japanese themes once again became popular among artists and craftsmen. Undoubtedly the most enduring theme was the four seasons. Here, a decorative snowflake pattern has been styled for textiles and lacquerware.

135 ■ Snow and Willow

Originally woven into the brocade for a Noh costume, this design of willow branches bending under the weight of newly fallen snow was typical of the poetic imagery popular in the last part of the period. The weaving texture here is created by crossing the weft and warp.

135

136 ▪ Snow on Bamboo Leaves
This highly imaginative design might be difficult to identify without a title. Mounds of snow cover splayed bamboo leaves while fat snow drops fall against an inky sky. The pointillist effect comes from *maki-e*, a decorative process used in the making of fine lacquerware.

137 ▪ *Kanoko-Shibori*
The illusion of a snow-dappled bamboo plant is created here by *kanoko-shibori*, a tie-dyeing process popular in the sixteenth century. Minute pulls of cloth were tied off with thread and then dyed, set, and untied, leaving a negative-positive pattern such as this one.

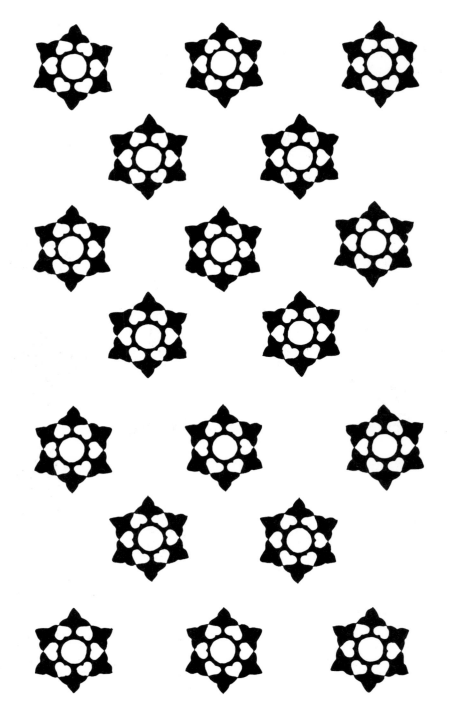

138

138 ■ Snow Crystals

Kamakuran commoners could not afford the expensive textiles worn by the samurai and courtiers, but they loved decorative patterns like this hexagonal snow ring design. This type of motif was simple to print, and everyone could afford the textiles it decorated.

139 ■ Oak Leaves

This simple motif of four oak leaves arranged within a star shape was easy to engrave and dye. Despite its winter look, its cheerful simplicity and generic personality made it a popular textile design for everyday clothing worn the year round.

140

140 ■ Mugworts and Irises

This pattern decorated *kosode* (small-sleeved kimono), first worn during the Kamakura period. These robes became popular because they reflected samurai austerity, and they were better suited to camp life than the trailing, open-sleeved robes of the Fujiwaras.

141 ■ Fern

Like the plum pattern, the fern motif is loved for its association with early spring. Here, it decorates a set of ceramic plates. Notice that on each of the six plates, the handpainted design is slightly different.

141

Descriptions of Color Plates

1 ■ Linked Gems and Maple
This elegant design of maple leaves drifting across a ground of soft geometry was first used to decorate a Noh costume in the Muromachi period (1338–1568). Early Noh theater dramatized ancient Japanese legends and was similar in tone to European medieval morality plays.

2 ■ Cherry Blossoms
This stylized design of weeping cherry decorated *kosode* (small-sleeved kimono). Heian women wore *kosode* as an undergarment, never seen outside the dressing room. The spartan camp life of Kamakuran society, on the other hand, called for simpler, more practical wear, and Kamakuran women wore *kosode* as everyday clothing.

3 ■ Tapir
This classic samurai pattern was taken from a *fubako* (a painted box used by a warrior in the field to store his letters and papers). The sleek image of a tapir is set in roundels on a tortoise shell ground. To the samurai, the tapir represented courage and cunning; the tortoise (believed then to live ten thousand years) promised longevity.

4 ■ Oda Nobunaga's Crest
Oda Nobunaga, mighty warrior and castle builder of the Momoyama period (1576–1603), owned this dramatically beautiful crest stamped onto a Chinese-inspired fretwork. The design is elegant, strong, and authoritative—all qualities that characterized Oda.

5 ■ Nature
The symmetry and imagery here suggest that this pattern was borrowed from a Chinese brocade. The Kamakura (1185–1338) and Muromachi periods saw a revived enthusiasm for all aspects of classical Chinese culture. Ironically, the zeal with which the Japanese embraced the Zen Buddhist qualities of selflessness and anti-materialism was matched by an ardent lust for Chinese brocades.

6 ■ Flower and Bird
The pure Chinese style evidenced in this pattern enjoyed a revival in the Kamakura period, thanks to Shogun Yoritomo. While rebuilding Tōdaiji, a famous Buddhist temple, the shogun's artisans were encouraged to study the Chinese arts and crafts of the T'ang dynasty. Owing to this reacquaintance with Chinese design, Kamakuran artisans incorporated these new/old ideas into their own painting, calligraphy, and lacquerware.

7 ■ First Plum Blossom
This beautiful design first appeared on the pottery of Nonomura Ninsei. The balance between the elements of *bu* and *bun* is symbolized by the fragility of the plum blossoms and the brute strength of the tree trunk. The samurai had a deep appreciation for such visual poetry and often decorated their personal possessions with similar metaphorical images.

8 ■ Checks and Clouds
The splendid Noh costumes that are used today are replicas of the court costume worn by officials during the Muromachi period. This handsome design of clouds floating on a subtle *ichimatsu* (checked) background is typical of the brilliant imported brocades that were used to make the glorious robes of the Noh actors and their privileged audience.

9 ■ Irises on Leather
Although we don't usually associate flowers with a warrior culture, the samurai often adopted a particular flower as their personal *mon* and used it to decorate their armor. Many of the great shoguns were renowned as much for their *ikebana* (flower arranging) as for their swordsmanship.

10 ■ Herringbone Drum and Peony
The elaborate design of drumheads and peonies on a herringbone ground originated with a textile used for Kamakuran court dress. Although simplicity was all-important in Yoritomo's warrior society,

ceremonial occasions still required the wearing of *uchikake*, a robe usually made from costly, imported brocades. The robe was worn with *hakama* (long, trailing trousers), and is still worn today for traditional festivals and Noh performances.

11 ■ *Kugi-Nuki* and *Unpan* on Chevrons

Textile artists often used imagery borrowed from architectural tools and details. This elegant design is composed of *kugi-nuki*, a tool used to remove nails from wooden planks, and *unpan*, an instrument used in Zen temples to call the priests to meals. This imagery, coupled with a patchwork of chevrons, was probably woven into a brocade of gold and silk.

12 ■ Irises and Water Reeds

The lining of a samurai's armor was made of painted leather pieces called *ekawa*. To soften it, the leather was repeatedly bleached in water and dried in the sun. This spare triangle design composed of irises and water reeds was originally painted onto softened leather dyed deep indigo. The leather industry was one of the few crafts to flourish during the Kamakura period. Others, such as weaving, almost died out for lack of patronage.

13 ■ Scattered Leaves

This shimmering tumble of autumn leaves decorated a samurai's saddle crafted during the Kamakura period. The leather was dyed, painted, and embellished with a process known as *raden* (mother-of-pearl inlay). The *raden* gives the design its pearly, iridescent coloring.

14 ■ Tree Bark

For decorating armor, the samurai favored either small geometric motifs (*komon*) or wandering stripes (*tatewaku*). The design often had a metaphorical importance germaine to the warrior's work. For example, this *tatewaku* stripe suggests tree bark—the kind of tough exterior a samurai needed for battle.

15 ■ Scattered Dragonflies

The dragonfly may not conjure up an image of strength, but it was often chosen to decorate a samurai's armor. Kamakuran society esteemed modesty and simplicity, virtues represented by the dragonfly, and considered the creature an appropriate talisman for battlefield and court, where samurai fashion was emulated.

16 ■ Flowers, Plants, and *Tanzaku*

This pattern includes images of water lilies and other pond plants floating around strips of *tanzaku*, the handmade paper traditionally used to write *tanka* verse. The choice of imagery suggests that these are romantic poems. The design probably comes from a Noh costume worn by the romantic heroine.

17 ■ Wisteria

The design of the Noh costume where this wisteria pattern originated was engineered to glorify the four seasons. Traditional Heian designs like this fell out of favor during the severe Kamakura period but were revived during the more relaxed Muromachi.

18 ■ Flowering Plants, *Tanzaku*, and *Yatsu-Hashi*

This flowering design of spring blooms, *tanzaku* (poetry papers), and *yatsu-hashi* (zigzag bridge) is typical of the lavish brocades collected by the Muromachi and Momoyama shoguns. Many of the most beautiful and expensive textiles were given to the shogun's favorite Noh actor and eventually became Noh costumes. Fragments of these fabrics have survived because each Noh school was an extended family that passed down its treasures from generation to generation.

■ GLOSSARY

Bakafu The term used to describe the administration of a military ruler. Originating in China, the word referred to the headquarters of the T'ang emperor's inner palace guards or the headquarters of a general on a military expedition. The term was borrowed by the Japanese in the tenth century and popularized by Yoritomo, the first shogun, who applied it to his military encampment in Kamakura. Gradually, *bakafu* came to mean both the residence and the organs of warrior government. Headed by the shogun, the *bakafu* was distinct from the imperial or court government.

Bu The martial arts (archery, swordsmanship, horsemanship, hunting, and falconry) as opposed to the literary and civilian arts of government and letters of *bun*.

Bun As opposed to *bu*, literary studies and civilian arts, including the courtly pursuits of calligraphy, *ikebana* (flower arranging), and *chanoyu* (tea ceremony).

Bushidō Literally, the Way of the Warrior. A martial ethic developed by the military that promised patronage by the lord in return for military service by the vassal. The warriors, with their distinctive culture, became their own social class known as samurai. They lived by the *bushidō* code, which demanded that they renounce all personal needs and desires to serve the needs and desires of their lord. The warrior ethic extolled the virtues of spartan living, physical endurance, and the willingness to die for one's lord.

Chanoyu Literally, "hot water for tea." The Japanese term for tea ceremony. Tea was brought to Japan from China before the tenth century, but the custom of tea drinking did not take hold until the diffusion of Zen Buddhism—also from China—in the thirteenth century. Initially, tea was served to guests in the Zen monasteries and used as a stimulant to help the monks endure long periods of meditation. The custom spread from the monasteries to the court, to the Kyoto merchants, and to the provincial warriors —who also patronized Zen. Along the way, a distinctive aesthetic of rustic sim-

plicity (*wabi*) was cultivated and is still studied as a ritual of hospitality today.

Courtiers The aristocratic class of Heian-kyō, who resided within the walls of the capital city. This group of several hundred nobles, palace ladies, and members of the imperial family—usually connected to the throne by birth or marriage —constituted a highly refined, leisured, and literary elite. Aristocratic business for the courtiers consisted of an appreciation of proper protocol and etiquette and a mastery of poetry writing, calligraphy, and music. Elegance and sensitivity were much more important than military and political skills, which were generally considered to be necessary but uncouth talents. At its best, this obsession with aesthetic refinement (*miyobi*) resulted in a fusion of life and art and stimulated an outpouring of artistic treasures that made the Heian period the golden age of Japan.

Daimyō Literally, "great name." Feudal lords who controlled Japan's provinces for more than seven hundred years and who were also great patrons and practitioners of the arts. During the fifteenth and sixteenth centuries (the Age of Wars), over 250 *daimyō* vied for local power. Oda Nobunaga initiated the reunification of Japan by attempting to bring all these warring factions together. Oda's work was carried on by Hideyoshi and completed by Tokugawa Ieyasu. Under the Tokugawa shogunate, a *daimyō* was defined as the lord of a domain who had an income of at least ten thousand *koku* (1 *koku* = five bushels of rice).

Edo period Long, stable, and peaceful Japanese historical era (1603–1868). In 1590, military ruler Tokugawa Ieyasu centered his *bakafu* (tent headquarters) in the remote provincial center of Edo (present-day Tokyo). Eventually, the economic and cultural center of the country shifted from Kyoto/Osaka to the Tokyo plain. The Edo period, which was free of influence from abroad because all foreigners were banned, was noted for its openness and creativity in society and the arts. Popular literature and art flourished in this time.

Ekawa Painted leather pieces. This beautifully decorated leather was used to line the inside of a warrior's armor. The leather was first washed, bleached, and worked until it was soft and supple. Finally, it was decorated by painting or stenciling, often with the warrior's personal pattern.

Fubako A letter box. Warriors used these to hold their personal papers and valuables. They were often made of lacquer and beautifully decorated.

Gagaku Elegant court music performed for its own sake or for the accompaniment of *bugaku* (court dances). Music was an important part of Heian life, and the courtiers were expected to be proficient on a variety of instruments, including the *biwa* and the *koto*.

Genji Tribal name of the Minamotos, a powerful military family that fought the Heike (Taira family) for control of the court in the late Heian period.

Hakama Full, trailing trousers resembling a divided skirt that were worn by men and women.

Heian period Japanese historical era (794–1185) noted for its extraordinary concern for beauty, delicacy, and sensitivity in life and the arts. In 794, the imperial court moved from Nara to Heian-kyō (the capital of peace and tranquility), which was renamed Kyoto 11 centuries later. Under the strong emperors Kammu and Saga during the early part of the Heian period (794–897), Japan maintained active relations with T'ang China. Then, as the powers of the emperors began to wane, one family of courtiers—the Fujiwaras—came to dominate affairs of state. After 894, communications with China were suspended, and the period from 897 to 1185 was called the late Heian, or Fujiwara, period. Japan then sought to develop its own artistic spirit. This shift of emphasis is clearly evident in the evolution of textile design and other arts.

Heike Tribal name for the Taira clan, a powerful military family led by Kiyomori. The Heike took control of the imperial court in the later part of the Heian period. Ironically, the most important legacy of

these military men was the exquisitely beautiful Heike *Lotus Sutra (Heike Nōgyō)*, commissioned by Kiyomori before the ultimate defeat of the Heike by their mortal enemies, the Genji (Minamotos).

Hitatare The samurai's large square-cut ceremonial coat made of silk ramie or hemp.

Ichimatsu A checker-board pattern named for the actor Sadokawa Ichimatsu.

Ikebana The art of flower arranging. One of the skills that Japanese women must learn to prepare themselves for marriage. There are many methods of *ikebana*, and many schools in Japan teach the different methods.

Jin-Baori A warrior's sleeveless camp coat, usually worn over armor. The coat was often decorated on the back with the warrior's *mon* (personal crest).

Kamakura period Japanese historical era (1185–1338) noted for its militaristic character. The artistically brilliant Heian period ended in 1185, when, after years of conflict, the Minamoto family defeated the rival Taira family, and military families began their rise to power. Although the imperial court remained in Kyoto, its influence was lessened, and Kamakura in eastern Japan was chosen as the seat of the shogunate. In the arts, the intricate and delicate Heian patterns gave way to the more practical camouflage patterns used to cover armor.

Kanji The Chinese system of writing composed of ideographs in which each character represents a specific idea. First used in China in 14 B.C., the language was systematized by the time it reached Japan by way of Korea in the fifth century. Initially, *kanji* was taught only to male children, causing it to develop as a public language associated with political and military concerns. Today, *kanji* is one of the three written languages taught throughout Japan. To read a newspaper with complete comprehension, it is said, the reader must recognize and understand ten thousand *kanji* characters.

Kanokō-shibori Fine-knotted tie-dyeing.

Kanō School Kanō Tanyu and members of the Kanō School painted for Tokugawa Ieyasu at Edo Castle and Nijo Castle in Kyoto. Attuned to the Ieyasu ideals of frugality and simplicity, this early work, which set the standard for the Edo period and all Japanese refined taste since, acknowledged the Chinese heritage but interpreted traditional themes in a manner that has become recognized as distinctly Japanese.

Karakusa Literally, scrolling vine. A sequential pattern that is systematically organized so it can be endlessly expanded. An arabesque motif particularly characteristic of Heian patterns, *karakusa* can be traced from Persia to India, China, Korea, and finally Japan.

Komon Literally, miniature patterns. The patterns can be quite large, for some reason, and still be called *komon*. Widely appreciated during the Heian period, *komon* reached the zenith of popularity in the Edo period, when master stencil cutters designed blades that enabled the artists to expand their repertory of designs.

Kosode A woman's kimono with a small sleeve opening and a narrow cuff. During the Heian period, the *kosode* was an undergarment worn beneath a wide-sleeved kimono. In the Kamakura period, the modest *kosode* was adopted as the standard dress by women because life was spartan and the elaborate layering of robes was impractical. In the Muromachi period, the *kosode* was worn like a coat over undergarments. Today, a version of the *kosode* is still worn by Japanese married women.

Kusube A dyeing technique used in the decoration of leather battle gear and leatherwear. The discovery of this technique allowed artisans to decorate leather armor with small, fine designs that became closely associated with the samurai class.

Kyōgen Literally, "mad words." A type of theater that developed along with Noh drama; it is usually performed, in fact, between the acts in a Noh performance for comic relief. Where Noh is primarily concerned with the spiritual world, Kyōgen deals with the material, down-to-earth, humorous world. Kyōgen plays usually have two or three characters, including either a *diamyō* and a servant or two priests. Unlike the slow-paced, mannered Noh, Kyōgen has a lot of action—almost slapstick—and the actors wear no masks.

Maki-e Literally, sprinkled picture. A late-Heian technique for decorating lacquerware in which gold and silver particles were sprinkled onto moist lacquer to achieve the design. Each lacquer layer—often 40 or more—was then sanded to even the surface and bring out the luster.

Minamoto See "Genji."

Momoyama period Japanese historical era (1576–1603) named after a castle built by unifying *daimyō* Hideyoshi Toyotomi. Hideyoshi stopped the building of temples and started the building of castles in Japan.

Mon Family crest.

Muromachi (or Ashikaga) period-
Japanese historical era (1338–1568) ruled by the Ashikaga family. In spite of civil wars, the arts flourished, and contacts with China and Korea were renewed.

Nara period Japanese historical era (710–794) in which Japan was united for the first time. The period was named after the city of Nara, which is considered the ancient-ancient capital of Japan (Kyoto is the ancient capital). During this period, the Japanese were deeply influenced socially and artistically by Buddhism and T'ang dynasty China.

Noh The classical masked dance theater first presented as medieval morality plays by priests and later taken over and developed by professional travelling troupes. Noh drama flowered during the Muromachi period when it enjoyed the patronage of the imperial court and the shogunate. The stories are taken from ancient religious works, mythology, and folk themes and are usually imbued with deep metaphysical overtones that serve to create intense masked-dance dramas. Kyōgen is performed between the acts in a Noh performance and serves as a relief from the dramatic tensions.

Nonomura Ninsei Most famous potter in seventeenth-century Kyoto.

Obi A sash or cummerbund worn with a kimono. There are as many kind of *obi* as there are fabrics, colors, and designs. The correct *obi* choice depends on the kimono, the season, the occasion, and the wearer's marital status. Often hand-woven, the *obi* itself is a work of art.

Oda Nobunaga See "Shogun."

Raden Lacquer and mother-of-pearl inlay. Often used to decorate lacquerware.

Samurai From the verb *saburau*, meaning "to serve." In the Heian period, the samurai were warrior guards used by the imperial court. The meaning of the term was gradually extended to encompass the provincial warriors as they became more important at the end of the Heian period. In the Kamakura, Muromachi, and Edo periods, "samurai" usually described those warriors who had rank or office in shogun or *daimyō* service.

Shintoism Literally, "the way of the gods." The native religion of Japan, based on the virtues of simplicity, purity, and cleanliness. In contrast to Buddhism, which entered Japanese culture in the Nara period, Shintoism is an optimistic, positive religion that teaches a reverence for nature. Followers of Shintoism believe that God inhabits all living things in the form of *kami* (spirits), who are worshipped in and out of Shinto shrines. The later spread of Confucianism and Buddhism lessened the influence of Shintoism, but the religion is still important in Japanese life; a large part of what we admire as "typically Japanese" is based on Shintoism.

Shogun A contraction of *seiitaishogun*, meaning "great general who quells the barbarians." Originally, shogun was a temporary title given to the princes who led military campaigns for the imperial court in the Heian period. The title took on great weight when it was awarded to Minamoto Yoritomo, founder of the Kamakura *bakafu*. After Yoritomo, it became customary for those warrior chieftains who established *bakafu* to assume the title of shogun as an expression of their legitimate authority as the military arm of imperial sovereignty.

Sung dynasty, Northern Chinese historical era (960–1126), which paralleled Japan's Heian period. More introspective than the extroverted T'ang dynasty that was the inspiration for most of Heian culture, the Sung dynasty is best known for its monochromatic ink landscapes. Still, many artistic devices that were important characteristics of Heian art—subdued color tones, bird's eye perspective, stress upon the diagonal plane—can be traced back to the Sung aesthetic.

T'ang dynasty Chinese historical era (618–906) known for its artistic creativity and cultural achievements. This was the golden age of Chinese poetry and the time of China's greatest influence on Korea and Japan.

Tanka A short poem consisting of five lines of 5, 7, 5, 7, and 7 syllables. From the tenth century, *tanka* became the favored form of verse and was practiced routinely by the educated classes, which included the samurai.

Tanzaku Handmade paper traditionally used to write *tanka* verse.

Tsujigahana-zome Stitched tie-dye that was a fashion in the Muromachi period.

Uchikake Long over-kimono worn by women, usually off the shoulders, for ceremonial occasions. These robes were often made of lavish brocades imported from China.

Waka Japanese poetry, each poem consisting of 31 syllables, written in *kana* script. *Waka* and *emaki-mono* were among the most important cultural achievements of the Heian period. The clandestine passing of *waka* poems was the preferred means of communication between the courtiers, who disliked direct communication. The making of this poetry was also an important social activity with the courtiers, who displayed their syllabic skills with the same intensity and enthusiasm that we might play tennis or croquet. The Heian aristocrat was far more likely to be judged by his poetic abilities than by his military talents.

Yoritomo See "Shogun."

Yukata An unlined cotton kimono worn by men, women, and children during the hot summer months. Usually block-printed or stenciled in blue-and-white patterns, these simple but functional garments are synonymous with summer relaxation and are usually worn at spas and in the home.

Zen One of the major traditions of Mahayana Buddhism that developed in China (as Chan) and flourished in Japan from its introduction there in the thirteenth century. Zen was embraced by the Kamakura shogunate because it stressed self-discipline, anti-materialism, and a spartan lifestyle—all of which appealed strongly to the emerging warrior class. Zen provided a powerful stimulus to the arts because it presented manual labor, secular literary and art forms, and meditation as possible vehicles for enlightenment.

BIBLIOGRAPHY

Baker, Joan Stanley. *Japanese Art.* London: Thames and Hudson, Ltd., 1984.

Collcutt, Martin, Marius Jansen, and Isao Kamakura. *Cultural Atlas of Japan.* New York: Facts on File, Inc., 1988.

Endo, Shusaku. *The Samurai.* Translated by Van G. Hessel. New York: Vintage Books, A Division of Random House, 1982.

Minnish, Helen Benton. *Japanese Costume.* Rutland, VT, and Tokyo: Charles E. Tuttle Co., 1963.

Shimizu, Yoshiaki (editor). *Japan: The Shaping of Daimyō Culture, 1185–1868.* New York: George Braziller, Inc., Publishers. Washington, DC: National Gallery of Art, 1988.

Yoshikawa, Eiji. *The Heike Story.* Translated by Fuki Wooyenaka Uramatsu. Rutland, VT, and Tokyo: Charles E. Tuttle Co., 1956.